THE EPIC MATCH

HERCULES

VS

THOR

by Claudia Oviedo

CAPSTONE PRESS
a capstone imprint

Published by Capstone Press, an imprint of Capstone
1710 Roe Crest Drive, North Mankato, Minnesota 56003
capstonepub.com

Library of Congress Cataloging-in-Publication Data is available
on the Library of Congress website
ISBN: 9781666343700 (hardcover)
ISBN: 9781666343724 (paperback)
ISBN: 9781666343731 (ebook PDF)

Summary:
It's a battle of the famous strongman versus the great protector.
The Roman god Hercules is known for his tremendous strength
and determination. The Norse god Thor is fearless and commands
lightning, thunder, and storms. If these two heroes were to battle, who
would come out on top?

Editorial Credits
Editor: Julie Gassman; Designer: Heidi Thompson; Media Researchers:
Jo Miller and Pam Mitsakos; Production Specialist: Tori Abraham

Image Credits
Alamy: Album, 18, CalimaX, 17, Charles Walker Collection, 23,
Chronicle, 21, INTERFOTO, 13, North Wind Picture Archives, 9,
pictureLux/The Hollywood Archive, 25, Universal Images Group
North America LLC, 15; Shutterstock: Alessandro Cristiano, 4,
Christos Georghiou, 11, IMG Stock Studio, 7, InnaFelker, Cover (Top),
Liliya Butenko, 5, 29, Liub Shtein, 27 (Right), maratr, 6, Mastering_
Microstock, 27 (Left), Matteo Provendola, Cover (Bottom), Maykova
Galina, 16, Natalia Mikhalchuk, 8, Sergej Razvodovskij, 28

TABLE OF CONTENTS

Words in **bold** are in the glossary.

THE STRONGMAN VS. THE PROTECTOR

Myths have told tales of great heroes throughout the ages. Few heroes are better known than Hercules and Thor. Hercules was one of the most popular of all **Greco-Roman** heroes. Thor was the **Norse** god of thunder.

Hercules had incredible physical strength. Thor was the protector of humankind. One was popular during the Roman era. The other was popular during the Viking Age. But both continue to live in our imaginations. We can thank comic books and movies for that.

Hercules

But what would happen if Hercules met Thor? Who do you think would win? Who was the greater god?

Thor

FACT

The word *myth* describes stories from ancient times. They are stories of gods, heroes, and events. Ancient peoples believed their myths were true.

WHERE DID THEY COME FROM?

Hercules was a **demigod**. His father was Zeus, king of the gods. His mother was a **mortal** woman named Alcmene. The gods believed a mortal would be their champion one day. Zeus tricked Alcmene into having his child. This fulfilled the **prophecy**.

To trick Alcmene, Zeus (above) disguised himself as her husband Amphitryon.

Hercules was not welcome in the land of the gods. Alcmene had to raise Hercules in a mortal family. The goddess Hera was angry her husband, Zeus, had a child with someone else. She wanted Hercules dead.

Hercules was not born with powers. Hera was tricked into nursing him. Her milk gave him great strength and speed. She later sent two serpents to strangle him in his cradle. Hercules strangled the giant snakes instead.

Hera

FACT

Hercules was a Roman name. His Greek name was Heracles.

Thor was the Norse god of lightning. He got his strength from his powerful family. His mother was the giantess Jörd. His father was the god Odin. He was chief of the gods.

Jotunheim and Asgard

Jörd lived in Jotunheim, home to the Jotun—giant beings that came before the gods. The land of the gods was called Asgard. Midgard was Earth.

Odin

Thor was a half giant. However, he was raised by Odin and his stepmother, the goddess Frigg. They lived in the land of the gods. They trained Thor in the ways of the gods. He would grow up to receive his father's throne.

Frigg was the Norse goddess of marriage.

THE HEROES' GREATEST FEATS

Hercules's greatest strength was his **determination**. In a well-known myth, Hercules completed 12 **feats** to get on Hera's good side. In his first feat, Hercules faced the Nemean lion.

He shot the large lion with an arrow. Then he attacked it with his club. However, the lion's golden fur could not be harmed by weapons. Finally, Hercules cornered the lion in a cave. He grabbed it by the neck and wrestled it to death.

The next 11 feats were just as hard. Hercules slayed a nine-headed **hydra**. He captured a mythical bull. He also stole a herd of man-eating mares from a king. Hercules never gave up.

FACT

Hercules skinned the dead
Nemean lion. He used one
of its claws to do it. He wore
the **hide** as armor.

Thor's greatest strength was being fearless. Many myths tell of his battles against giants. In one he fights Hrungnir, the mightiest of all the giants. The other giants did not want Hrungnir to lose and make them look bad. They made a huge giant out of clay to frighten Thor.

On the day of the duel, Thor was not afraid. He flung Mjolnir, his magical hammer, hard and far. It struck Hrungnir in the head and killed him instantly. The clay giant was the one who was scared. He even wet himself.

Thor's Treasures

Thor had several magical items. Mjolnir, Thor's hammer, could only be held and used by someone worthy. It always returned when thrown. Megingjord, his belt, doubled Thor's strength. Járngreipr, his iron gloves, helped Thor control his hammer.

Although Hrungnir (far left) was the mightiest of giants,
Thor (right) easily defeated him with the help of his hammer.

HOW THEY FAILED

Hercules's temper was his greatest weakness. In one myth, Hera did not like seeing Hercules happy with a family. She punished him with madness. During that madness, Hercules didn't recognize his wife and children. He thought they were strangers in his home and killed them.

Hercules's half sister, the goddess Athena, knocked him out with a stone. When Hercules woke up, he was filled with grief. He hadn't realized what he was doing.

Athena often helped Hercules, including during three of his 12 feats.

This was not the only time Hercules killed someone because of his temper. As a young man, Hercules hit his music teacher with a lyre during an argument. The small harp killed the teacher. Hercules didn't know his own strength yet. His quick temper always got him in trouble.

Hercules's physical strength became a weakness when he could not control it.

The giant king Utgard-Loki also went by the name Skrymir.

Thor's greatest weakness was being too trusting. This made him easy to trick. One myth told of Thor's journey to Utgard-Loki's castle in Jotunheim. The giant king who lived there challenged Thor to a drinking contest. Thor was given a giant horn and told to finish in three gulps. He drank and drank but could not empty the horn.

One myth says when Utgard-Loki slept, his snoring created earthquakes.

Next, the giant king challenged Thor to lift a cat. The cat arched his back. Thor couldn't lift him. Thor demanded a fight. The giant king had him face an old woman. She brought Thor down to a single knee.

Thor and his companions spent the night at the castle. Then, the giant king admitted that he had tricked Thor in each of his challenges.

When Thor drank from the horn, it was lowered into the sea. The cat Thor tried to lift was the Midgard Serpent. It was a giant serpent wrapped around the Earth. The old woman was actually Old Age. No one can defeat old age. Thor had been tricked again and again.

FACT
Which day of the week is named after Thor? Thursday!

HEROES' ENDS

Hercules was born mortal, but death made him a god. Greco-Roman myth says that when he died, it was by accident. One day, Hercules's second wife heard he might be falling in love with someone else. She gave him a tunic. She'd been told this long shirt was **enchanted** with a love potion. She just wanted Hercules to love her again.

However, the tunic was poisoned by one of his enemies. It burned Hercules. The pain was so bad that he built himself a funeral **pyre**. Then, he threw himself on the bonfire.

The goddess Athena had a soft spot for Hercules. She carried him to Olympus on her chariot. They rose to the heavens, and he became a full god.

The poison on the tunic that killed Hercules was the blood of a centaur, a mythical creature that is half man and half horse.

Thor is a god, but he can still die just like everyone else. Norse myth **foretells** that he will die in battle at Ragnarök. Ragnarök is a series of events that will lead to the end of the world.

The Midgard Serpent will unwrap itself from the Earth. This movement will cause earthquakes and other natural disasters. The serpent and an army of other giants will invade Asgard. They will try to destroy the world and kill many gods.

Thor will fight them. The serpent will poison the sky with its breath. Thor will crush the serpent with his powerful hammer. It will die. Then, Thor will choke on the poison. He will turn, take nine steps, and fall. He will die too.

The killing of the serpent and the death of Thor is the last event in the great battle of the gods at Ragnarök.

LEGENDS NEVER DIE

Hercules continues to be well-known. There are at least 19 Italian movies about him. Hollywood has made more than 20 movies and TV shows. He is also a character in more than a dozen video games. Various songs name him. This includes music from the Broadway show *Hercules*. It is based on an animated Disney film.

The god of war has a minor role in various DC Comics series. He also joins Thor as a Marvel Avenger in the comic books.

FACT
The fifth-largest constellation in the sky is named Hercules.

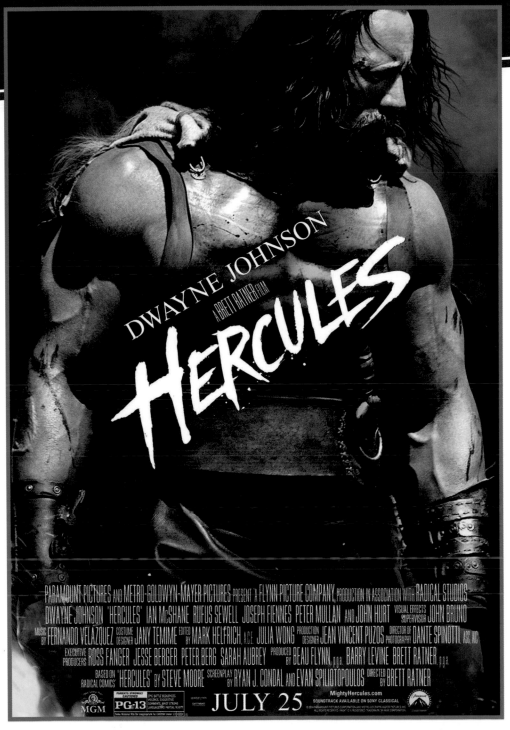

Dwayne (The Rock) Johnson starred in the 2014 movie, *Hercules*.

Thor is also well-known today. A chemical **element**, Thorium, is named after him. Thor also appears in video games and at least one TV series. Versions of him appear in many books, including Rick Riordan's Percy Jackson and the Olympians series.

Comics have made Thor even more popular. There is a Marvel comic based on him, and he is a Marvel Avenger. Several hit movies also feature the god of thunder.

Hercules and Thor came from different cultures and different times. Modern versions of the heroes allow us to imagine a battle between the two.

How would you end their fight?

Hercules

Thor

HERCULES VS. THOR AT A GLANCE

Name:	Hercules
God of:	War
Appearance:	Bronze-skinned, muscular, and has a beard
Weapons:	A club and the Nemean lion's skin, which acts like armor
Strength:	Determination
Powers and abilities:	He has amazing strength, stamina, and endurance.
Weakness:	Short temper
Symbol:	A wooden club

Name:	Thor
God of:	Thunder
Appearance:	Large and muscular; traditionally, he has long, red hair and a red beard. Marvel gave him blond hair.
Weapon:	A hammer called Mjolnir
Strength:	Fearlessness
Powers and abilities:	He has incredible strength and can throw his hammer extremely far. He commands lightning, thunder, and storms.
Weakness:	Too trusting
Symbol:	His hammer

GLOSSARY

demigod (DEM-ee-god)—a child of a god and a human

determination (dih-tur-muh-NAY-shun)—the state of having a firm goal

element (EL-uh-muhnt)—a basic substance in chemistry that cannot be split into simpler substances

enchanted (en-CHANT-ed)—under a spell or magical

feat (FEET)—an action that requires courage and talent

foretell (FOR-tell)—to tell of something beforehand or to predict

Greco-Roman (gree-koh-ROH-muhn)—coming from both Greek and Roman cultures

hide (HYDE)—the skin of an animal

hydra (HYE-druh)—a many-headed serpent or monster in Greek mythology

mortal (MOR-tuhl)—a human who will eventually die

Norse (NORS)—related to ancient Scandinavia

prophecy (PROF-uh-see)—a prediction about the future

pyre (PYE-ur)—a pile of wood for burning a dead body

READ MORE

Briggs, Korwin. *Gods and Heroes: Mythology Around the World*. New York: Workman Publishing, 2018.

Marcus, Richard, Natalie Buczynsky, and Jonathan Shelnutt. *Introduction to Greek Mythology for Kids: A Fun Collection of the Best Heroes, Monsters, and Gods in Greek Myth*. Berkeley: Ulysses Press, 2021.

Nordvig, Mathias. *Norse Mythology for Kids: Tales of Gods, Creatures, and Quests*. Emeryville, CA: Rockridge Press, 2020.

INTERNET SITES

Ancient Greek Gods for Kids: The 12 Labors of Hercules
greece.mrdonn.org/greekgods/hercules.html

National Geographic Kids: The Gods and Goddesses of Ancient Greece!
natgeokids.com/uk/discover/history/greece/greek-gods/

The Vikings: Gods and Myths
vikings.mrdonn.org/gods.html

INDEX

ABOUT THE AUTHOR

Claudia Oviedo writes for children under various names. Reading about different mythologies with her kids is a favorite pastime. Claudia has received several honors for her work. They include 2009 Paterson Prize for Books for Young People, as well as the 2008 and 2015 Texas Institute of Letters Best Young Adult Book Award, and several starred reviews for her picture books.